FEARLESS
CONVERSATION™

HOW CAN WE BE FULLY FAITHFUL WHEN WE'RE FULLY FLAWED?

**DISCUSSIONS FROM
1-2 SAMUEL, 1 CHRONICLES, PSALMS**

PARTICIPANT GUIDE

Loveland, CO

Group
Real. **Bold.** Love.

Group resources really work!

This Group resource incorporates our R.E.A.L. approach to ministry. It reinforces a growing friendship with Jesus, encourages long-term learning, and results in life transformation, because it's:

Relational—Learner-to-learner interaction enhances learning and builds Christian friendships.

Experiential—What learners experience through discussion and action sticks with them up to 9 times longer than what they simply hear or read.

Applicable—The aim of Christian education is to equip learners to be both hearers and doers of God's Word.

Learner-based—Learners understand and retain more when the learning process takes into consideration how they learn best.

Fearless Conversation: How Can We Be Fully Faithful When We're Fully Flawed?
Discussions from 1-2 Samuel, 1 Chronicles, Psalms
Participant Guide

Visit our website: **group.com**

Fearless Conversation adult Sunday school curriculum is created by the amazing adult ministry team at Group. Contributing writers for this quarter are:

Larry Shallenberger • Amy Simpson • Thomas Smith • Jill Wuellner

Photos © dreamstime.com

Unless otherwise indicated, all Scripture quotations are taken from the *Holy Bible*, New International Version® NIV® Copyright © 1973, 1978, 1984, 2011 by Biblica, Inc.® Used by permission. All rights reserved worldwide.

978-1-4707-1680-6
Printed in the United States of America.

10 9 8 7 6 5 4 3 2 1   21 20 19 18 17 16 15 14

CONTENTS

HERE'S WHAT A LESSON LOOKS LIKE

Your leader will guide each lesson through four sections:

GREETING

Make new friends and start the conversation as the topic of the week is introduced.

GROUNDING

This is where you read the Scripture for the week. The Bible content is always provided here in the participant guide. After hearing God's Word read aloud, you'll have the opportunity to follow the inductive study method of writing down first responses, questions, thoughts, or ideas that are sparked by the Bible reading.

GRAPPLING

Here's where the conversation deepens. You'll find questions that are intentionally challenging to answer. These won't have easy answers and you won't have a fill-in-the-blank option. Everyone will wrestle with the questions that the lesson provides, as well as their own questions that they're wondering about. The leader will ask God to guide the conversation—and you can join in that prayer! Remember to treat others with respect during these conversations, even if you don't agree with them. Listen first. Speak second.

GROWING

Here's where the personal application comes in. You'll have the chance to reflect on what God's Word, as shared in this lesson, means to you for your own life and determine what your personal response is.

Throughout each lesson you'll also find two other helps:

BEHIND THE SCENES

These sections of commentary and notes from Bible scholars will give you additional context into history, language, culture, and other relevant information. You can read these sections ahead of time or during the lesson—whichever works best for you.

GOING DEEPER

These tips will help you be a great conversationalist. They remind you how to keep a conversation going, how to be a better listener, and how to be respectful even if you don't agree with someone.

FINAL TIP:

Have a sense of divine anticipation. Approach each class with a heart full of anticipation over what God might do that day. God is alive and present with you and your class. Always prepare by praying, asking God to help you see his hand at work in the conversation. Trust God to show up and show you and others in the class exactly where he wants the conversation to go!

EARLESS
NVERSATION™

HOW CAN WE BE
FULLY FAITHFUL
WHEN WE'RE
FULLY FLAWED?

LESSON 1: WHAT DOES IT MEAN THAT "THE LORD LOOKS AT THE HEART"?

GREETING

What is your best quality?

Thoughts about the person in the picture:

Do you think God cares about our physical appearance?

LESSON 1: WHAT DOES IT MEAN THAT
"THE LORD LOOKS AT THE HEART"?

7

GROUNDING

God's Word: 1 Samuel 16:1-13

[1] The Lord said to Samuel, "How long will you mourn for Saul, since I have rejected him as king over Israel? Fill your horn with oil and be on your way; I am sending you to Jesse of Bethlehem. I have chosen one of his sons to be king."

[2] But Samuel said, "How can I go? If Saul hears about it, he will kill me."

The Lord said, "Take a heifer with you and say, 'I have come to sacrifice to the Lord.' [3] Invite Jesse to the sacrifice, and I will show you what to do. You are to anoint for me the one I indicate."

[4] Samuel did what the Lord said. When he arrived at Bethlehem, the elders of the town trembled when they met him. They asked, "Do you come in peace?"

[5] Samuel replied, "Yes, in peace; I have come to sacrifice to the Lord. Consecrate yourselves and come to the sacrifice with me." Then he consecrated Jesse and his sons and invited them to the sacrifice.

[6] When they arrived, Samuel saw Eliab and thought, "Surely the Lord's anointed stands here before the Lord."

[7] But the Lord said to Samuel, "Do not consider his appearance or his height, for I have rejected him. The Lord does not look at the things people look at. People look at the outward appearance, but the Lord looks at the heart."

▶

⁸ Then Jesse called Abinadab and had him pass in front of Samuel. But Samuel said, "The Lord has not chosen this one either." ⁹ Jesse then had Shammah pass by, but Samuel said, "Nor has the Lord chosen this one." ¹⁰ Jesse had seven of his sons pass before Samuel, but Samuel said to him, "The Lord has not chosen these." ¹¹ So he asked Jesse, "Are these all the sons you have?"

"There is still the youngest," Jesse answered. "He is tending the sheep."

Samuel said, "Send for him; we will not sit down until he arrives."

¹² So he sent for him and had him brought in. He was glowing with health and had a fine appearance and handsome features.

Then the Lord said, "Rise and anoint him; this is the one."

¹³ So Samuel took the horn of oil and anointed him in the presence of his brothers, and from that day on the Spirit of the Lord came powerfully upon David. Samuel then went to Ramah.

What are the first questions that come to mind about this passage? What jumps out at you and catches your attention?

Capture those thoughts here.

LESSON 1: WHAT DOES IT MEAN THAT "THE LORD LOOKS AT THE HEART"?

9

GRAPPLING

GOING DEEPER

You can help others in your group go deeper by listening with your full attention and by asking questions as others share. Saying "I wonder about what you just said. Tell me more!" will help people know you care about what they're saying and want them to open up more.

BEHIND THE SCENES

It's important to understand the history of Israel and the way it was ruled to appreciate what happened in 1 Samuel 16:1-13. Israel was unique in that it was a nation that didn't have an earthly king. Israel's king was God himself, speaking to his people through prophets, defending them through a series of judges, and spiritually guiding them through the priests. In David's time, this judge, prophet, and priest was Samuel. But with a desire to be like other nations, Israel demanded a physical, human king. God relented, and instructed Samuel to anoint tall and handsome Saul as Israel's first king. But Saul had a prideful heart and, ultimately, didn't trust God. In fact, he blatantly disobeyed him, leading God to reject Saul and send Samuel to Jesse's house to anoint David as Israel's new king. And although it would be years until David actually became king, God knew David's heart was faithful and obedient. He wasn't perfect, as we'll see in future lessons, but his heart was always for God, which made all the difference.

> You'll find "Behind the Scenes" boxes with Bible commentary provided throughout this lesson. You can read these ahead of time or as you move through the lesson. They're there to help you gain a better understanding of the Bible.

What's the difference between "intention" and "desire" of the heart? How does sin affect the way these are displayed?

God saw David's heart, just like he sees yours. David wasn't perfect. He sinned, just like we all do. What did God see in David that set him apart from everyone else?

BEHIND THE SCENES

While many of us think of David as a king, what else do we know about him? He was the eighth son of Jesse, who was the grandson of Ruth and Boaz. Interestingly, when Samuel told Jesse to bring his sons for the anointing, David was not included. That, coupled with David acting as the family shepherd, has led some to speculate that David wasn't seen as very important within his family. He would have spent his days—and possibly his nights—outdoors, enjoying nature while caring for his sheep. Not only did he lead them to pastures and streams, but he also defended them against bears and lions that would attack his flock (1 Samuel 17:34-35).

The exact age of David at the time of this account is not known, but it is generally assumed that he was a teenager. He took the throne from Saul at the age of 30 after living in Saul's home, first to soothe Saul's nerves with his harp and then as a high ranking official in the army. He then endured years on the run, hiding from the king who wanted to kill him. It wasn't until Saul's death that David assumed the throne as king of Israel.

Why does it matter that God regularly chooses the unlikely hero?

INTERESTING THOUGHTS SPARKED
BY OTHERS IN MY GROUP:

BEHIND THE SCENES

When Samuel arrives in Bethlehem, he instructs the elders to "consecrate themselves," leaving them to perform the cleansing ritual in preparation for a sacrifice. Meanwhile, he goes to Jesse's home and takes on the responsibility of consecrating Jesse's family. It's possible that Jesse was a prominent member of the community, so this wouldn't have been unusual. But the real reason for the consecration was to give Samuel the opportunity to find the new king and anoint him secretly. God used the truth of Samuel's sacrifice to hide the anointing from Saul, thus protecting the lives of David and Samuel.

GROWING

BEHIND THE SCENES

"The Lord looks at the heart" (1 Samuel 16:7). There are several words in the Bible that are translated "heart." The Greek word *kardia* is used exclusively in the New Testament and specifically refers to the heart as the organ inside our bodies. The Hebrew word *lebab* is the word used in 1 Samuel 16:7 and means the inner man, mind, will, and heart.

What does God see when he looks at your heart? Pride or humility? The desire to follow him or do your own thing?

Write your reflections here.

HOW CAN WE BE
FULLY FAITHFUL
WHEN WE'RE
FULLY FLAWED?

LESSON 2: WHAT DO I DO WHEN GOD'S PEOPLE ARE ENEMIES OF EACH OTHER?

GREETING

What is the hardest thing you've ever had to learn how to do?

How do you think this activity of moving the can relates to conflict in our lives?

GROUNDING

God's Word: 1 Samuel 18:5-16

[5] Whatever mission Saul sent him on, David was so successful that Saul gave him a high rank in the army. This pleased all the troops, and Saul's officers as well.

[6] When the men were returning home after David had killed the Philistine, the women came out from all the towns of Israel to meet King Saul with singing and dancing, with joyful songs and with timbrels and lyres. [7] As they danced, they sang: "Saul has slain his thousands, and David his tens of thousands."

[8] Saul was very angry; this refrain displeased him greatly. "They have credited David with tens of thousands," he thought, "but me with only thousands. What more can he get but the kingdom?" [9] And from that time on Saul kept a close eye on David.

[10] The next day an evil spirit from God came forcefully on Saul. He was prophesying in his house, while David was playing the lyre, as he usually did. Saul had a spear in his hand [11] and he hurled it, saying to himself, "I'll pin David to the wall." But David eluded him twice.

PARTICIPANT GUIDE

¹² Saul was afraid of David, because the Lord was with David but had departed from Saul. ¹³ So he sent David away from him and gave him command over a thousand men, and David led the troops in their campaigns.

¹⁴ In everything he did he had great success, because the Lord was with him. ¹⁵ When Saul saw how successful he was, he was afraid of him. ¹⁶ But all Israel and Judah loved David, because he led them in their campaigns.

What are the first questions that come to mind? What jumps out at you and catches your attention?

Capture those thoughts here.

GRAPPLING

GOING DEEPER

We're all different. Some of us like to speak up, and some of us are more reserved. Some are more familiar with the Bible than others. Some need lots of processing time, and others quickly connect the dots or reach a conclusion. We have different experiences and questions. And…we can learn from one another! Learn from others and let others learn from you by asking questions and sharing with respect for one another.

BEHIND THE SCENES

In the culture of David and Saul, it was common for women and children to celebrate the return of a victorious army by welcoming them home with a triumphal entry. They would fill the streets with singing, dancing, and music in a kind of ancient ticker-tape parade. In this way they would honor the men who had led the army into victory. Unfortunately, the song these women sang was more honoring to David, the shepherd boy, than to Saul, their king. While it's true David's action of killing Goliath led to the defeat of the Philistine army, he, himself, did not kill tens of thousands. Was it wise for this song to be sung in the presence of the king? Probably not, as the result was to injure his pride and give rise to his feelings of jealousy.

Compare and contrast the way Saul and David handled this situation. What stands out to you?

What might have happened if David had sought revenge on Saul? Why is it so important that he didn't?

INTERESTING THOUGHTS SPARKED
BY OTHERS IN MY GROUP:

BEHIND THE SCENES

First Samuel 16:14 says, "The Spirit of the Lord had departed from Saul, and an evil spirit from the Lord tormented him." Then in chapter 18 verse 10 it says, "The next day an evil spirit from God came forcefully on Saul. He was prophesying in his house, while David was playing the lyre, as he usually did. Saul had a spear in his hand...."

What does that mean? Prior to Christ's return to heaven in the New Testament, the Holy Spirit's presence was not for salvation, but it was a guide to those chosen by God to lead his people. When God removed his Spirit from Saul, he essentially removed his guidance and protection. God never initiates evil, but God did allow an evil spirit to come upon Saul. This spirit could have been what led Saul to "prophesy." The way the sentence is written in Hebrew suggests that Saul "pretended to prophesy," either in an effort to deceive David, or simply because Saul was agitated. Whatever the reason, the result wasn't good.

What caused all of this activity between David and Saul to happen?

How do you know God was in control of this incident and allowed it to happen?

BEHIND THE SCENES

It wouldn't have been unusual for Saul to have had a javelin close at hand at all times. In fact, during this time in history a king didn't hold a scepter but a javelin, or spear, which was the sign of kingly authority. The javelin is actually an older symbol of royalty than a crown. In ancient times, the javelin was more like a walking stick that the king would use to rest or lean upon. Roman emperors were the first to begin adding symbolic emblems to the tops of their staffs, adding such things as globes and eagles. It wasn't until Tarquin the Elder, the fifth king of Rome (who ruled from 616 B.C. to 579 B.C.) that kings started carrying what we know today as a scepter.

GROWING

BEHIND THE SCENES

First Samuel 18:14 says, "In everything he [David] did he had great success, because the Lord was with him." The word "success" comes from the Hebrew word *sakal*, which can also be translated as "wisdom" or "prospered." Even though Saul tried to kill David by javelin and by placing him in battle (verse 13), God had chosen David as king. His presence was the reason David gained such success and popularity and was also the reason Saul was so afraid of him.

How do you deal with conflict? Do you gossip and try to get others on your side, or do you respond in love? Do you let God defend you?

Write your reflections here.

EARLESS
ONVERSATION™

**HOW CAN WE BE
FULLY FAITHFUL
WHEN WE'RE
FULLY FLAWED?**

LESSON 3: IS IT OKAY TO COMPLAIN TO GOD IN PRAYER?

GREETING

Other than people telling you to do silly relay races, what are some things that are easy to complain about?

How would you feel if you had to use that object? What if you had to see it or use it every day?

How do you think this change in perspective might relate to our topic of complaining to God?

GROUNDING

God's Word: Psalm 142

A maskil of David. When he was in the cave. A prayer.

[1] I cry aloud to the Lord;
    I lift up my voice to the Lord for mercy.
[2] I pour out before him my complaint;
    before him I tell my trouble.

[3] When my spirit grows faint within me,
    it is you who watch over my way.
In the path where I walk
    people have hidden a snare for me.
[4] Look and see, there is no one at my right hand;
    no one is concerned for me.
I have no refuge;
    no one cares for my life.

[5] I cry to you, Lord;
    I say, "You are my refuge,
    my portion in the land of the living."

[6] Listen to my cry,
    for I am in desperate need;

rescue me from those who pursue me,
  for they are too strong for me.
⁷ Set me free from my prison,
  that I may praise your name.
Then the righteous will gather about me
  because of your goodness to me.

What were you feeling when you first read this Scripture? Did you gain any comfort or peace from these words? Anything in particular catch your attention?

Capture those thoughts here.

$\mathcal{G}$RAPPLING

GOING DEEPER

Many times Christians won't express their doubts and questions because they don't feel like it's safe to do so—that perhaps they'll be seen as some sort of heretic. Resolving our doubts is a great way to strengthen faith, so give people all kinds of room, grace, and mercy when they start asking questions about matters of faith that might be fully resolved in your own mind.

BEHIND THE SCENES

The word "psalms" is actually from the Greek word *psalmos*, which is a song accompanied by stringed instruments. In English we have come to understand *psalms* as "a song of praise" without musical accompaniment. Either way, the book of Psalms is a series of poems emphasizing the writer's emotions to God...emotions of praise and adoration as well as fears and doubt. Interestingly, there isn't one psalm of lament that doesn't move from focusing on present trouble to praising God.

The author of Psalms is typically attributed as David. While it's believed David wrote 73 of the psalms, some are credited as being written by Moses and Solomon, as well as three Levite musicians: Asaph, Heman the Ezrahite, and Ethan the Ezrahite.

What does David tell you about God in this psalm?

Why is it important that David specifically says he is complaining to God and that he is complaining out loud?

BEHIND THE SCENES

What is a "maskil" anyway? It's a term used in the title of 13 of David's psalms, and the word has, in some Bible versions, been translated as "with understanding" or "in a skillful psalm." It's generally understood that this term indicates the psalm is for instruction. It's possible that with this psalm, David was instructing others how to pray during times of trouble based on the lessons he learned while hiding in the cave.

Why did God allow David, his chosen king, to endure such hardship for so many years?

PARTICIPANT GUIDE

BEHIND THE SCENES

Psalm 142 notes that it was written "in the cave," as if everyone knows the cave to which David's referring. There are two times in the Bible when David was in a cave while running for his life. In 1 Samuel 22 David ran to the Cave of Adullam, and while it's not specifically known where this cave is, it's thought to be located about 2 miles south of where David killed Goliath. Then in 1 Samuel 24 David and his men are hiding in the Desert of En-Gedi, an oasis on the western shore of the Dead Sea. Saul went to find David with every intention of killing him. When Saul went into a cave to rest, David was hiding in that very cave and secretly cut off a piece of Saul's robe. It's not known specifically which cave David was in when he wrote Psalm 142, but many believe it was the Cave of Adullam, as it seems David was alone when this prayer was offered to God.

GROWING

What about you? What troubles are on your heart? Where do you need help from God?

Write a prayer asking God for the help you need right now.

**HOW CAN WE BE
FULLY FAITHFUL
WHEN WE'RE
FULLY FLAWED?**

LESSON 4: WHAT IS GOD'S ROLE IN WAR AND POLITICS?

GREETING

If you were to start your own political party, what would you call it?

Write the name of your new political party on your name tag.

How will God's role be depicted in your museum? Will God be given a special exhibit? A little space in every exhibit? No space at all? Consider how God's place in politics and history should be shown.

How might God's role in war and politics look different in the Bible than in your museum?

GROUNDING

God's Word: 2 Samuel 5:1-10

¹All the tribes of Israel came to David at Hebron and said, "We are your own flesh and blood. ²In the past, while Saul was king over us, you were the one who led Israel on their military campaigns. And the Lord said to you, 'You will shepherd my people Israel, and you will become their ruler.'"

³When all the elders of Israel had come to King David at Hebron, the king made a covenant with them at Hebron before the Lord, and they anointed David king over Israel.

⁴David was thirty years old when he became king, and he reigned forty years. ⁵In Hebron he reigned over Judah seven years and six months, and in Jerusalem he reigned over all Israel and Judah thirty-three years.

⁶The king and his men marched to Jerusalem to attack the Jebusites, who lived there. The Jebusites said to David, "You will not get in here; even the blind and the lame can ward you off." They thought, "David cannot get in here." ⁷Nevertheless, David captured the fortress of Zion—which is the City of David.

▶

⁸ On that day David had said, "Anyone who conquers the Jebusites will have to use the water shaft to reach those 'lame and blind' who are David's enemies." That is why they say, "The 'blind and lame' will not enter the palace."

⁹ David then took up residence in the fortress and called it the City of David. He built up the area around it, from the terraces inward. ¹⁰ And he became more and more powerful, because the Lord God Almighty was with him.

What went through your mind as you read this account? What impressions of David did you get? Is there something here you question?

Capture those thoughts here.

GRAPPLING

(left margin, vertical) PARTICIPANT GUIDE

GOING DEEPER

You can help your whole group go deeper if you're brave enough to ask the questions everyone is thinking about but others are afraid to ask. Don't worry about sounding "stupid" or being labeled a "doubter." Others will be relieved you brought up the question so you can all look for answers.

BEHIND THE SCENES

David had already been selected by God and anointed by Samuel as a young boy, and he was ready to assume the throne when Saul died. So why did he need all the tribes of Israel to affirm his authority as king?

After Saul's death, only one tribe (Judah) accepted David as king. The other tribes elevated Saul's fourth son, Ish-bosheth, as king. Two men loyal to David murdered Ish-bosheth as he was sleeping and brought his head to David, expecting a reward. Instead, David had the men put to death for killing an innocent man (2 Samuel 4).

Now that Ish-bosheth was dead, the rogue tribes of Israel had no king to lead them and no hope of maintaining a separate kingdom. So they agreed to unite with Judah and honor David as their king.

The tribes of Israel gave three reasons for submitting to David's kingship: David was an Israelite like them; David had a long history of leading the Israelites to military victory; David was chosen by God to lead his people.

David's great and history-making rule over Israel began with this unification of the tribes.

BEHIND THE SCENES

Bible scholars have long puzzled over the meaning of mentioning "the blind and the lame" in this passage. It simply is not clear what the Jebusites and King David meant by these references. Some believe the Jebusites were so confident in Jerusalem's strength that they placed blind and disabled men up on their walls as a taunt to David's army.

This viewpoint suggests that when David spoke of "those 'lame and blind' who are David's enemies," he was referring to those men who were defending the city wall.

It's also possible that the Jebusites spoke symbolically, referring to their warriors as "lame and blind" to make the point that even warriors who could not see or walk would be successful in defending the city against David's soldiers. Either way, the Jebusites unwisely failed to take the threat seriously.

How is God's role visible in 2 Samuel's description of David's consolidation of power?

BEHIND THE SCENES

This occasion marked the third time David was anointed as king.

The first time was when he was an adolescent, when Samuel came to his father under God's guidance and selected him among his brothers. This first anointing was kept secret and did little to change David's everyday life, since Saul was the official king of Israel at that time. But it must have done something to David's heart and his sense of courage. After all, David was a young man of faith, and he now knew he had been selected by God to lead his people.

The second anointing came when the tribe of Judah (David's own tribe) made him their king at Hebron. This was after Saul's death, when the other tribes were loyal to Saul's son Ish-Bosheth. This anointing was an act of bold defiance by the tribe of Judah, and it led to war between their tribe and the others.

This third anointing also took place at Hebron. But this time it was neither contested nor secret. It was cause for a great celebration, as it symbolized the unification of the tribes into one kingdom. The people of Israel held a three-day feast, with more than 300,000 men from all 12 tribes participating.

In what ways does God's power often remain hidden in political situations? Can you think of some specific examples?

INTERESTING THOUGHTS SPARKED
BY OTHERS IN MY GROUP:

What is the relationship between God's presence and political or military success?

⎰G R O W I N G

BEHIND THE SCENES

It's interesting David had to conquer the city of Jerusalem and take it from the Jebusites, considering the people of Israel had already conquered the city after Joshua's death and still possessed it during Saul's reign. It's not clear how or when they lost the city to the Jebusites.

Some commentators believe the Jebusites were able to capture Jerusalem during a time of weakness after King Saul's death, while David and the tribe of Judah were at war with Saul's son Ish-bosheth and the remaining tribes, who were loyal to him.

With your small group, think of at least one current political event happening in our world. Talk about how God might be working in, through, and around that event.

As you talk with your group, write your group's thoughts here.

**HOW CAN WE BE
FULLY FAITHFUL
WHEN WE'RE
FULLY FLAWED?**

LESSON 5: WHY IS GOD SO VIOLENT?

GREETING

Why do you think war is such a common theme in our culture?

What is it that makes some people want to celebrate violence?

GROUNDING

God's Word: Psalm 21

For the director of music. A psalm of David.

[1] The king rejoices in your strength, Lord.
How great is his joy in the victories you give!

[2] You have granted him his heart's desire
and have not withheld the request of his lips.
[3] You came to greet him with rich blessings
and placed a crown of pure gold on his head.
[4] He asked you for life, and you gave it to him—
length of days, for ever and ever.
[5] Through the victories you gave, his glory is great;
you have bestowed on him splendor and majesty.
[6] Surely you have granted him unending blessings
and made him glad with the joy of your presence.
[7] For the king trusts in the Lord;
through the unfailing love of the Most High
he will not be shaken.

[8] Your hand will lay hold on all your enemies;
your right hand will seize your foes.

[9] When you appear for battle,
you will burn them up as in a blazing furnace.
The Lord will swallow them up in his wrath,
and his fire will consume them.
[10] You will destroy their descendants from the earth,
their posterity from mankind.

36 FEARLESS CONVERSATION: **HOW CAN WE BE FULLY FAITHFUL WHEN WE'RE FULLY FLAWED?**

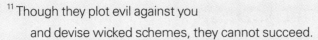

¹¹ Though they plot evil against you

and devise wicked schemes, they cannot succeed.

¹² You will make them turn their backs

when you aim at them with drawn bow.

¹³ Be exalted in your strength, Lord;

we will sing and praise your might.

What are the first questions that come to mind? What are your first impressions, feelings, or insights?

Capture those thoughts here.

RAPPLING

GOING DEEPER

You can help others in your group go deeper if you don't let anyone get away with a "yes" or "no" answer. Always follow up by asking, "What led you to that thought?" or "Can you tell us more?"

BEHIND THE SCENES

Psalm 21 is not just a celebration of David's military victory. Most Bible scholars believe this psalm is at least partially messianic in nature, meaning it refers to the Messiah, Jesus, who would be born as a descendant of King David. Some believe the entire psalm is referring only to Jesus himself, while others believe David refers to both himself and the coming Messiah.

Ancient Jewish scholars understood the king in Psalm 21 to be the coming Messiah; this view was changed in the Middle Ages in an effort to avoid reinforcing the Christian view that this psalm presents a picture of Jesus.

David's psalms commonly include prophecies about the coming Messiah, and David himself served as a symbol of that eternal King who would come after him. Verse 4 is an example of what is probably a dual meaning: "He asked you for life, and you gave it to him—length of days, for ever and ever." David received eternal life through his faith in God and the coming Messiah, and Jesus' reign would last forever. This verse applies to both of them.

"He will not be shaken" is an example of a phrase that probably applies to the coming Messiah, whose reign would never end, rather than to David. However, since Jesus would be born as a descendant of David, it also applies to David's symbolic reign through Jesus. God had given David this promise through the prophet Nathan: "Your house and your kingdom will endure forever before me; your throne will be established forever" (2 Samuel 7:16). This prophecy was fulfilled in Jesus.

How would you describe God as portrayed in this psalm?

Why did David rejoice in seeing other people destroyed by violence?

INTERESTING THOUGHTS SPARKED
BY OTHERS IN MY GROUP:

BEHIND THE SCENES

At face value, it may appear as if David was thanking God for giving him decisive victory over his enemies. But there's more going on here. A closer look at David's words reveals that he was rejoicing over the defeat not of his enemies, but of God's enemies.

Verse 8 tells us, "Your hand will lay hold on all your enemies; your right hand will seize your foes."

So who are God's enemies? Verse 11 tells us the defeated ones "plot evil against" God and "devise wicked schemes." They intentionally rebelled against God, God's plans, and God's people. The defeated people were not innocent victims; they were paying for crimes against God. God used his people to exercise his judgment.

While we might be uncomfortable with the idea of a loving God destroying people, we must remember how grateful we feel when God stops the work of evil people. In verse 11 David praised God because the people who plotted evil in rebellion against God "cannot succeed." This should bring us great comfort.

God is, without question, kind and loving and patient. But God is also terrifying and perfect in judgment. Like David, we can and should stand in awe of this aspect of God's goodness.

How and why might God choose to do his work through violence?

BEHIND THE SCENES

Just as the conquered enemies mentioned in this psalm were God's enemies, the victory was God's as well. David's focus was on God's strength, not on his own. David did not lead his army for his own sake; he was an agent of God. He did not lead in his own power; he was empowered by God. And he knew where to give the glory when the battle was over. This did not diminish David's joy; in fact, he took great joy in praising God's great strength and mighty acts.

GROWING

BEHIND THE SCENES

The Prophet Samuel called David "a man after [God's] own heart" (1 Samuel 13:14). This psalm is just one of the many places where David revealed that heart. Despite his imperfections and failings, David knew God. And nothing gave him more joy than God himself.

While David was enthusiastic in thanking God for military victory, his greater source of joy was in God's "unending blessings," "the joy of [God's] presence," and God's "unfailing love" (verses 6-7). God himself was enough for David to rejoice and commit that he and his people would continue to praise God and sing of his might.

How has violence hurt you and people you love?

Write your reflections here.

How has God worked through violence to protect or provide for you and people you love?

Write your thoughts here.

What will you thank or ask God for?

Write your reflections here.

HOW CAN WE BE FULLY FAITHFUL WHEN WE'RE FULLY FLAWED?

LESSON 6: DAVID WAS A LIAR, ADULTERER, AND MURDERER...SO WHY IS HE A HERO OF OUR FAITH?

GREETING

What does it take to overcome a flaw?

Why do great leaders often fall from grace?

GROUNDING

God's Word: 2 Samuel 11:1-27

[1] In the spring, at the time when kings go off to war, David sent Joab out with the king's men and the whole Israelite army. They destroyed the Ammonites and besieged Rabbah. But David remained in Jerusalem.

[2] One evening David got up from his bed and walked around on the roof of the palace. From the roof he saw a woman bathing. The woman was very beautiful, [3] and David sent someone to find out about her. The man said, "She is Bathsheba, the daughter of Eliam and the wife of Uriah the Hittite." [4] Then David sent messengers to get her. She came to him, and he slept with her. (Now she was purifying herself from her monthly uncleanness.) Then she went back home. [5] The woman conceived and sent word to David, saying, "I am pregnant."

[6] So David sent this word to Joab: "Send me Uriah the Hittite." And Joab sent him to David. [7] When Uriah came to him, David asked him how Joab was, how the soldiers were and how the war was going. [8] Then David said to Uriah, "Go down to your house and wash your feet." So Uriah left the palace, and a gift from the king was sent after him. [9] But Uriah slept at the entrance to the palace with all his master's servants and did not go down to his house.

[10] David was told, "Uriah did not go home." So he asked Uriah, "Haven't you just come from a military campaign? Why didn't you go home?"

[11] Uriah said to David, "The ark and Israel and Judah are staying in tents, and my commander Joab and my lord's men are camped in the open country. How could I go to my house to eat and drink and make love to my wife? As surely as you live, I will not do such a thing!"

¹² Then David said to him, "Stay here one more day, and tomorrow I will send you back." So Uriah remained in Jerusalem that day and the next. ¹³ At David's invitation, he ate and drank with him, and David made him drunk. But in the evening Uriah went out to sleep on his mat among his master's servants; he did not go home.

¹⁴ In the morning David wrote a letter to Joab and sent it with Uriah. ¹⁵ In it he wrote, "Put Uriah out in front where the fighting is fiercest. Then withdraw from him so he will be struck down and die."

¹⁶ So while Joab had the city under siege, he put Uriah at a place where he knew the strongest defenders were. ¹⁷ When the men of the city came out and fought against Joab, some of the men in David's army fell; moreover, Uriah the Hittite died.

¹⁸ Joab sent David a full account of the battle. ¹⁹ He instructed the messenger: "When you have finished giving the king this account of the battle, ²⁰ the king's anger may flare up, and he may ask you, 'Why did you get so close to the city to fight? Didn't you know they would shoot arrows from the wall? ²¹ Who killed Abimelek son of Jerub-Besheth? Didn't a woman drop an upper millstone on him from the wall, so that he died in Thebez? Why did you get so close to the wall?' If he asks you this, then say to him, 'Moreover, your servant Uriah the Hittite is dead.'"

²² The messenger set out, and when he arrived he told David everything Joab had sent him to say. ²³ The messenger said to David, "The men overpowered us and came out against us in the open, but we drove them back to the entrance of the city gate. ²⁴ Then the archers shot arrows at your servants from the wall, and some of the king's men died. Moreover, your servant Uriah the Hittite is dead."

²⁵ David told the messenger, "Say this to Joab: 'Don't let this upset you; the sword devours one as well as another. Press the attack against the city and destroy it.' Say this to encourage Joab."

²⁶When Uriah's wife heard that her husband was dead, she mourned for him. ²⁷After the time of mourning was over, David had her brought to his house, and she became his wife and bore him a son. But the thing David had done displeased the Lord.

What are the first questions that come to mind? What impressions do you have of David?

Capture those thoughts here.

BEHIND THE SCENES

Up until this point David's life has been one long series of successes and honors. From defeating the giant Goliath to being made king, David seems to lead a charmed life. But beginning with the section we are examining today, that all changes when King David turns to lust and other sins. Because of his giving in to sin, David begins to shirk his duties as both king and military leader during a time of battle. In fact, while his troops are off fighting the Ammonites, he sends Joab off to fight in his place while he stays behind.

Consequently, the account in 2 Samuel 11:1-27 chronicles David's negligence of his duty, his adultery with Bathsheba, and the murder of Uriah. His spiritual lack of self-control had clear physical ramifications. He neglected his duties, developed lazy habits, and his all-consuming lust led to violence, deceit, and the death of an innocent man. The ultimate result: His sinful actions displeased God and resulted in a series of divine punishments and the death of his son.

PARTICIPANT GUIDE

GRAPPLING

GOING DEEPER

Look around to see if there's anyone new in class who you haven't met. If so, be sure to offer that person a warm welcome and help them feel at home. You may want to sit with that person and introduce them to others in the class.

BEHIND THE SCENES

Second Samuel 11:1-27 gives us a rather simplified look at a very complex life. And it also shows how one action leads to another. For example, the passage begins with these words: "In the spring, at the time when kings go off to war, David sent Joab out with the king's men and the whole Israelite army. They destroyed the Ammonites and besieged Rabbah. But David remained in Jerusalem." Here in modern-day America, spring means the beginning of baseball season. In David's day, spring was the beginning of *go conquer a neighboring region* season. Okay, that might be stretching a point. But in all seriousness, during David's time the beginning of spring was the time when kings led their armies into battle. But instead of leading the army himself, David sent Joab. So while his men risked their lives on the battlefield, David chose to stay in Jerusalem. And it was during this time that he saw Bathsheba.

What do you find most shocking about this incident in David's life, and why?

Why do you think David went to such extreme lengths to cover up his actions with Bathsheba? What was his motivation for the cover-up?

What does David's story tell us about how God still works through flawed leaders?

INTERESTING THOUGHTS SPARKED
BY OTHERS IN MY GROUP:

Why did David's sins keep progressing to more sin? How is this like what happens in our own lives?

BEHIND THE SCENES

Up to this point in his life, David was often called a "man after God's own heart," but to the best of our knowledge he is never referred to that way again after the events recorded in these passages. And even though God forgave David and he continued as king, his life was never the same. There were still repercussions associated with his sin, and the results of his sin plagued him for years. The child he fathered with Bathsheba died. And his bad example as a father was not lost on his sons. Amnon raped his half-sister, and Absalom rebelled against David and tried to take his kingdom from him.

GROWING

BEHIND THE SCENES

David, for all his previously devout life, does not come to the realization that he needs forgiveness on his own. It is only after he is confronted by the prophet Nathan about his sin that he asks for God's forgiveness. After his meeting with Nathan, David composes Psalm 51, saying: "Have mercy on me, O God, according to your unfailing love; according to your great compassion blot out my transgressions. Wash away all my iniquity and cleanse me from my sin" (Psalm 51:1-2). (We'll discuss David's full prayer for forgiveness in Psalm 51 in greater detail during the next lesson.)

When in your life have you allowed your desires to override what you knew was right?

Write your thoughts here.

What do you need to do to move from the sins of your past to allow God to lead you for the future?

Write your ideas here.

HOW CAN WE BE FULLY FAITHFUL WHEN WE'RE FULLY FLAWED?

LESSON 7: IF GOD FORGIVES ME, THEN WHY DO I STILL GET PUNISHED FOR MY SINS?

GREETING

When was a time that you, as a child or as a teenager, did something wrong and had to face the consequences?

Why do you think we do wrong things, when we know we might get caught and have to face the consequences?

BEHIND THE SCENES

As a prophet, Nathan was required to confront sin, even the sin of a king. It took great courage and discernment to approach David with his wrongdoings. When Nathan confronted David about the death of Uriah, he did it in the form of a story. He wanted to "ease" David into the realization of what he had done. But hot-headed David flew into a rage and said that any man in his kingdom who would do such a thing was worthy of death and would be executed. Nathan then pointed his finger at David and said, "Thou art the man!"

And the shoe, as they say, was suddenly on the other foot. At that point David understood that God knew what he had done and the consequences were coming.

GROUNDING

God's Word: Psalm 51

PARTICIPANT GUIDE

[1] Have mercy on me, O God,
    according to your unfailing love;
according to your great compassion
    blot out my transgressions.
[2] Wash away all my iniquity
    and cleanse me from my sin.

[3] For I know my transgressions,
    and my sin is always before me.
[4] Against you, you only, have I sinned
    and done what is evil in your sight;
so you are right in your verdict
    and justified when you judge.

▼

⁵Surely I was sinful at birth,

 sinful from the time my mother conceived me.

⁶Yet you desired faithfulness even in the womb;

 you taught me wisdom in that secret place.

⁷Cleanse me with hyssop, and I will be clean;

 wash me, and I will be whiter than snow.

⁸Let me hear joy and gladness;

 let the bones you have crushed rejoice.

⁹Hide your face from my sins

 and blot out all my iniquity.

¹⁰Create in me a pure heart, O God,

 and renew a steadfast spirit within me.

¹¹Do not cast me from your presence

 or take your Holy Spirit from me.

¹²Restore to me the joy of your salvation

 and grant me a willing spirit, to sustain me.

¹³Then I will teach transgressors your ways,

 so that sinners will turn back to you.

¹⁴Deliver me from the guilt of bloodshed, O God,

 you who are God my Savior,

 and my tongue will sing of your righteousness.

¹⁵Open my lips, Lord,

 and my mouth will declare your praise.

¹⁶You do not delight in sacrifice, or I would bring it;

 you do not take pleasure in burnt offerings.

¹⁷My sacrifice, O God, is a broken spirit;

 a broken and contrite heart

 you, God, will not despise.

¹⁸May it please you to prosper Zion,

 to build up the walls of Jerusalem.

¹⁹Then you will delight in the sacrifices of the righteous,

 in burnt offerings offered whole;

 then bulls will be offered on your altar.

What are the first questions that come to mind? What sort of jumps out at you and catches your attention?

Capture those thoughts here.

GRAPPLING

GOING DEEPER

You can help your group go deeper by how you handle disagreements. If you have a difference of opinion with someone, saying, "I'm not sure I agree. Can you help me understand?" goes a long way to show you respect their opinion, even if you don't share it.

BEHIND THE SCENES

In Psalm 51 the Greek word *metanoia* is used to indicate true repentance: a change of mind and purpose and life. In this sense, David is conscious of his guilt and helplessness to do anything about his past sins on his own. He is at the mercy of God.

David realizes that true repentance consists of 1) a true sense of one's own guilt and sinfulness; 2) a desire for God's mercy; and 3) a heartfelt desire to live a holy life.

From this account in Psalm 51, what can we learn about God's desire to forgive?

Why does David say he has only sinned against God?

INTERESTING THOUGHTS SPARKED
BY OTHERS IN MY GROUP:

BEHIND THE SCENES

Even though David faced his sins following Nathan's confrontation and asked God to forgive him, things didn't end there. David could see his faults and readily admitted them. And while David was forgiven, his house would continue to display the sins he had sought to cover.

David's life and family were never the same as a result of what he had done. Murder was a constant threat in his family, his household rebelled against him, his wives were given to someone else, and his first child by Bathsheba died.

Do you think David was bargaining with God? Explain your answer, and tell if you think this is a good idea or not.

GROWING

BEHIND THE SCENES

Because we are born sinful (Psalm 51:5), our natural tendency is to please ourselves rather than God. David followed that pattern when he decided to take another man's wife. David also discovered what he needed to do to make his heart right with God. Right behaviors come out of a right heart.

David prayed for cleansing from his sin. Hyssop was a plant used by the priest in Old Testament ceremonial laws to symbolize the cleansing of sin. In his prayer David cried, "Restore to me the joy of your salvation." He understood that unconfessed sin makes intimacy with God impossible. The message of this psalm is evidence that David's prayer was answered.

My personal psalm for forgiveness and restoration:

PARTICIPANT GUIDE

HOW CAN WE BE FULLY FAITHFUL WHEN WE'RE FULLY FLAWED?

LESSON 8: WHAT DO I DO WITH MY SORROW?

GREETING

BEHIND THE SCENES

Absalom wanted not merely to succeed his father as king, but to replace his father while he was still reigning. Through manipulation and political scheming, he managed to gain the support of a large contingent. Absalom then moved to Hebron, the previous capital city of Judah, and declared himself king. That action triggered a civil war between himself and his father (2 Samuel 15:1-12). The attempted coup was so successful at the beginning that David had to flee from Jerusalem to Mahanaim, across the Jordan.

Absalom then took over the throne in Jerusalem. It looked like the end for David, except that God had already decided who would succeed David on the throne. And it wasn't Absalom. Soon Absalom and his followers proved to be no match for David's army and Absalom lost 20,000 of his troops. The rest ran away.

PARTICIPANT GUIDE

Should we try to avoid sadness in our lives? Explain your answer.

What are some negative ways people deal with grief or sadness?

What are some positive ways people deal with grief or sadness?

GROUNDING

God's Word: 2 Samuel 18:9–19:8

⁹ Now Absalom happened to meet David's men. He was riding his mule, and as the mule went under the thick branches of a large oak, Absalom's hair got caught in the tree. He was left hanging in midair, while the mule he was riding kept on going.

¹⁰ When one of the men saw what had happened, he told Joab, "I just saw Absalom hanging in an oak tree."

¹¹ Joab said to the man who had told him this, "What! You saw him? Why didn't you strike him to the ground right there? Then I would have had to give you ten shekels of silver and a warrior's belt."

▶

¹² But the man replied, "Even if a thousand shekels were weighed out into my hands, I would not lay a hand on the king's son. In our hearing the king commanded you and Abishai and Ittai, 'Protect the young man Absalom for my sake.' ¹³ And if I had put my life in jeopardy—and nothing is hidden from the king—you would have kept your distance from me."

¹⁴ Joab said, "I'm not going to wait like this for you." So he took three javelins in his hand and plunged them into Absalom's heart while Absalom was still alive in the oak tree. ¹⁵ And ten of Joab's armor-bearers surrounded Absalom, struck him and killed him.

¹⁶ Then Joab sounded the trumpet, and the troops stopped pursuing Israel, for Joab halted them. ¹⁷ They took Absalom, threw him into a big pit in the forest and piled up a large heap of rocks over him. Meanwhile, all the Israelites fled to their homes.

¹⁸ During his lifetime Absalom had taken a pillar and erected it in the King's Valley as a monument to himself, for he thought, "I have no son to carry on the memory of my name." He named the pillar after himself, and it is called Absalom's Monument to this day.

¹⁹ Now Ahimaaz son of Zadok said, "Let me run and take the news to the king that the Lord has vindicated him by delivering him from the hand of his enemies."

²⁰ "You are not the one to take the news today," Joab told him. "You may take the news another time, but you must not do so today, because the king's son is dead."

²¹ Then Joab said to a Cushite, "Go, tell the king what you have seen." The Cushite bowed down before Joab and ran off.

²² Ahimaaz son of Zadok again said to Joab, "Come what may, please let me run behind the Cushite."

But Joab replied, "My son, why do you want to go? You don't have any news that will bring you a reward."

²³ He said, "Come what may, I want to run." So Joab said, "Run!" Then Ahimaaz ran by way of the plain and outran the Cushite.

²⁴ While David was sitting between the inner and outer gates, the watchman went up to the roof of the gateway by the wall. As he looked out, he saw a man running alone.

²⁵ The watchman called out to the king and reported it. The king said, "If he is alone, he must have good news." And the runner came closer and closer.

²⁶ Then the watchman saw another runner, and he called down to the gatekeeper, "Look, another man running alone!" The king said, "He must be bringing good news, too." ²⁷ The watchman said, "It seems to me that the first one runs like Ahimaaz son of Zadok."

"He's a good man," the king said. "He comes with good news."

²⁸ Then Ahimaaz called out to the king, "All is well!" He bowed down before the king with his face to the ground and said, "Praise be to the Lord your God! He has delivered up those who lifted their hands against my lord the king."

²⁹ The king asked, "Is the young man Absalom safe?" Ahimaaz answered, "I saw great confusion just as Joab was about to send the king's servant and me, your servant, but I don't know what it was." ³⁰ The king said, "Stand aside and wait here." So he stepped aside and stood there.

³¹ Then the Cushite arrived and said, "My lord the king, hear the good news! The Lord has vindicated you today by delivering you from the hand of all who rose up against you."

³² The king asked the Cushite, "Is the young man Absalom safe?" The Cushite replied, "May the enemies of my lord the king and all who rise up to harm you be like that young man." ³³ The king was shaken. He went up to the room over the gateway and wept. As he went, he said: "O my son Absalom! My son, my son Absalom! If only I had died instead of you—O Absalom, my son, my son!"

19. Joab was told, "The king is weeping and mourning for Absalom." ² And for the whole army the victory that day was turned into mourning, because on that day the troops heard it said, "The king is grieving for his son." ³ The men stole into the city that day as men steal in who are ashamed when they flee from battle. ⁴ The king covered his face and cried aloud, "O my son Absalom! O Absalom, my son, my son!"

⁵ Then Joab went into the house to the king and said, "Today you have humiliated all your men, who have just saved your life and the lives of your sons and daughters and the lives of your wives and concubines. ⁶ You love those who hate you and hate those who love you. You have made it clear today that the commanders and their men mean nothing to you. I see that you would be pleased if Absalom were alive today and all of us were dead. ⁷ Now go out and encourage your men. I swear by the Lord that if you don't go out, not a man will be left with you by nightfall. This will be worse for you than all the calamities that have come on you from your youth till now."

⁸ So the king got up and took his seat in the gateway. When the men were told, "The king is sitting in the gateway," they all came before him. Meanwhile, the Israelites had fled to their homes.

What are the first questions that come to mind? What is your reaction to what's happening in David's life?

Capture those thoughts here.

GRAPPLING

GOING DEEPER

Remember, the measure of a fearless conversation isn't whether or not you convince others of your opinions concerning the Bible. A fearless conversation is successful when the group collectively grows closer to God and each other.

BEHIND THE SCENES

Absalom was the third son of David. He was born at Hebron to David's third wife Maacah (the daughter of Talmai, king of Geshur). Absalom is described in 2 Samuel 14:25-27 in great detail: "In all Israel there was not a man so highly praised for his handsome appearance as Absalom. From the top of his head to the sole of his foot there was no blemish in him. Whenever he cut the hair of his head—he used to cut his hair once a year because it became too heavy for him—he would weigh it, and its weight was two hundred shekels [about 5 pounds] by the royal standard."

Oddly enough, Absalom's name means *father of peace*. His life, on the other hand, did not mirror his name. For example: David's oldest son, Amnon, assaulted Absalom's half-sister Tamar (2 Samuel 13-1-22). Absalom took a while to plot his revenge, but when the opportunity arose two years later during the sheep shearing time at Baal Hazor, Absalom had his brother Amnon killed (2 Samuel 13:23-29).

Do you feel David's reaction to his son's death was appropriate or inappropriate for the circumstances? Explain your reasoning.

Joab had to force David into action to keep his men from turning away from him. Why might it be important for us to continue moving forward in times of grief—or do you think Joab was wrong?

INTERESTING THOUGHTS SPARKED
BY OTHERS IN MY GROUP:

BEHIND THE SCENES

The consequences of David's sin unfold in the book of 2 Samuel. Through the grief and trials of his life, David learns an important principle: Godliness does not guarantee an easy and carefree life. One person who caused David grief was his third son, Absalom. Absolom incited the entire nation to rebellion and crowned himself king.

In Absalom, David saw a bitter replay of his own past sins. Nathan's predictions that David's family would suffer because of his sin against Bathsheba and Uriah were coming true. David's love was rejected by Absalom. David also had to deal with the pain of a child who disobeyed God and was out of control.

How can we best deal with the sorrow that the messy parts of life bring our way?

GROWING

BEHIND THE SCENES

When David's first son from Bathsheba died, his immediate response was to go to the temple and worship. He did not continue to dwell on his sin. He turned to God and was renewed to start his life over. With God's forgiveness he was to move past his sorrow. Soon after that David and Bathsheba gave birth to another son, Solomon (2 Samuel 12:21-23).

What in your life is causing you grief or sorrow? What has been your response to those emotions?

Write your thoughts here.

How can your relationship with God help you find healing? What will you do to make that happen?

Write your reflections here.

**HOW CAN WE BE
FULLY FAITHFUL
WHEN WE'RE
FULLY FLAWED?**

LESSON 9: HOW DO I HANDLE BETRAYAL?

GREETING

BEHIND THE SCENES

Psalm 41:9 has often been viewed as a prophecy of Christ's betrayal (John 13:18). Judas spent three years with Jesus as one of his disciples. He traveled with Jesus, learned from him, and served the cause by handling the group's finances. Judas knew Jesus very well. Eventually it was Judas who betrayed Jesus for the price of 30 pieces of silver. Even Jesus was not immune from the betrayal of a friend.

How did you feel sharing something that was not true about yourself?

Why is it often difficult to move past the hurt of betrayal?

PARTICIPANT GUIDE

GROUNDING

God's Word: Psalm 41

[1] Blessed are those who have regard for the weak;
    the Lord delivers them in times of trouble.
[2] The Lord protects and preserves them—
    they are counted among the blessed in the land—
    he does not give them over to the desire of their foes.
[3] The Lord sustains them on their sickbed
    and restores them from their bed of illness.

[4] I said, "Have mercy on me, Lord;
    heal me, for I have sinned against you."
[5] My enemies say of me in malice,
    "When will he die and his name perish?"
[6] When one of them comes to see me,
    he speaks falsely, while his heart gathers slander;
    then he goes out and spreads it around.

[7] All my enemies whisper together against me;
    they imagine the worst for me, saying,
[8] "A vile disease has afflicted him;
    he will never get up from the place where he lies."
[9] Even my close friend,
    someone I trusted,
one who shared my bread,
    has turned against me.

▶

¹⁰ But may you have mercy on me, Lord;
 raise me up, that I may repay them.
¹¹ I know that you are pleased with me,
 for my enemy does not triumph over me.
¹² Because of my integrity you uphold me
 and set me in your presence forever.

¹³ Praise be to the Lord, the God of Israel,
 from everlasting to everlasting.

Amen and Amen.

What are the first questions that come to mind? What do you find most interesting in David's prayer to God? What catches your attention?

Capture those thoughts here.

GRAPPLING

GOING DEEPER

Remember that just as you are responsible for your own learning, you can also play an important role in the faith journey of others. You can help others in your group go deeper by listening with your full attention and by asking questions as others share. Make this an interactive time together. Encouraging others will help people know you care about what they're saying and may help them open up more.

BEHIND THE SCENES

Psalm 41 paints a picture of a man at a turning point in his life. He has betrayed the trust of those he was empowered to rule, he has betrayed his close friends and advisors, and he has betrayed those who wanted nothing more than to serve their king. In the process he has been betrayed by his own son and has been put in the position of almost having his own army turn against him.

In short, David is at the end of his rope. His current circumstance has literally made him sick, and in his desperation (and his acceptance for what he's brought on himself) he asks God to forgive and restore him. In his prayer, he confesses his sins, acknowledges that God is unhappy with him, and realizes that he can only be restored again to God's favor by God's forgiveness.

From this psalm, it's not clear if David is physically sick and being betrayed while on his sickbed or if he has become sick over the betrayal of those close to him. When have you experienced physical discomfort because you were emotionally hurt by someone?

Why would God allow such things as betrayal to happen to those who serve him?

Do you think God ever feels betrayed by us? Explain your reasoning.

BEHIND THE SCENES

In verse 3 David writes: "The Lord sustains them on their sickbed and restores them from their bed of illness." The word he uses is *hapak*, which is translated as "restore." While this particular usage refers to the restoration of David's life, it can also be used to indicate a drastic change in direction. For example, God turning the Nile into a river of blood (Exodus 7:17, 20) and turning our sorrow into joy (Jeremiah 31:13, Psalm 30:11). For our purposes, *hapak* indicates a radical turn of events and a complete redemptive change.

What advise can we give each other on how to cope when we're betrayed by a friend or family member?

BEHIND THE SCENES

In the psalm, David makes two basic requests (see verse 10). First, he asks God to raise him up, give him his health, and have mercy on him. Then he asks to do to his enemies what they have done to him. Yet he doesn't want payback. This is different than revenge. His enemies are God's enemies, and he still wants to be victorious over them as was his original aim.

PARTICIPANT GUIDE

GROWING

BEHIND THE SCENES

Psalm 41 reminds us that sin and suffering are closely related. Sin in many ways has less to do with us—and the actual sinful action—than with our relationship to God. Because all sin is directed toward God, whether knowingly or unknowingly, it speaks to the need to confess our shortcomings to God. So David's statement "I have sinned" is the essence of true repentance.

It's interesting that David feels his sin as almost a living thing. Some translations (the Revised Standard Version, for example) translate verse 8 as, "A deadly thing has fastened upon him; he will rise not again from where he lies." The *deadly thing* is translated "a thing of Belial" (a Hebrew word that became "the personification of evil" in Jewish and Christian usage). The Gospel equivalent is: "He casts out demons by Beelzebub, the prince of demons" (Matthew 12:25-29; Mark 3:23-27; Luke 11:17-22).

What in your life needs to be confessed to God? (verse 4)

Write your reflections here.

What in your life pleases God? (verse 11)

Write your thoughts here.

How can your life praise God for the mercy he's shown you? (verse 13)

Write your ideas here.

FEARLESS CONVERSATION™

HOW CAN WE BE FULLY FAITHFUL WHEN WE'RE FULLY FLAWED?

LESSON 10: HOW CAN I KNOW, AND PURSUE, GOD'S PLAN FOR MY FAMILY'S FUTURE?

GREETING

The Three Pigs: A Parenting Parable

The Big, Bad Wolf: What bad influences do you fear might negatively influence your children?

The House of Straw: What's the worst collection of parenting strategies you can think of to shelter our children from harmful influences?

PARTICIPANT GUIDE

The House of Wood: What are some commonly held "pretty good" parenting strategies—maybe strategies that most parents use whether they are connected to God or not?

The House of Brick: What do you think are the best parenting strategies needed to help our children grow up to be adults who love God and their neighbors while escaping the negative influences that are out there?

GROUNDING

God's Word: 1 Chronicles 17:1-15

[1] When David was settled in his palace, he summoned Nathan the prophet. "Look," David said, "I am living in a beautiful cedar palace, but the Ark of the lord's Covenant is out there under a tent!"

[2] Nathan replied to David, "Do whatever you have in mind, for God is with you."

[3] But that same night God said to Nathan,

[4] "Go and tell my servant David, 'This is what the lord has declared: You are not the one to build a house for me to live in. [5] I have never lived in a house, from the day I brought the Israelites out of Egypt until this very day. My home has always been a tent, moving from one place to another in a Tabernacle. [6] Yet no matter where I have gone with the Israelites, I have never once complained to Israel's leaders, the

shepherds of my people. I have never asked them, "Why haven't you built me a beautiful cedar house?"'

[7] "Now go and say to my servant David, 'This is what the lord of Heaven's Armies has declared: I took you from tending sheep in the pasture and selected you to be the leader of my people Israel.[8] I have been with you wherever you have gone, and I have destroyed all your enemies before your eyes. Now I will make your name as famous as anyone who has ever lived on the earth! [9] And I will provide a homeland for my people Israel, planting them in a secure place where they will never be disturbed. Evil nations won't oppress them as they've done in the past, [10] starting from the time I appointed judges to rule my people Israel. And I will defeat all your enemies.

"'Furthermore, I declare that the lord will build a house for you—a dynasty of kings! [11] For when you die and join your ancestors, I will raise up one of your descendants, one of your sons, and I will make his kingdom strong. [12] He is the one who will build a house—a temple—for me. And I will secure his throne forever. [13] I will be his father, and he will be my son. I will never take my favor from him as I took it from the one who ruled before you. [14] I will confirm him as king over my house and my kingdom for all time, and his throne will be secure forever.'"

[*]So Nathan went back to David and told him everything the lord had said in this vision.

What are the first questions that come to mind? What jumps off the page at you? Where do you see God offering his help to David's descendants?

Capture those thoughts here.

BEHIND THE SCENES

The books of Chronicles could be called "A Tale of Two Houses." The storyline centers around David's house and God's house. The Chronicles seem to be organized around the idea that the wellbeing of the house of David rose and fell on its ability to honor God's house. The narrative this week is one of the pivotal moments in the book. Early in his reign, King David had brought the Ark of the Covenant to Jerusalem. However, he housed the Ark of the Covenant in a tent while he built an elaborate palace for himself. David wanted to rectify the situation by building a temple dedicated to worshipping God. He consulted Nathan the prophet who initially blessed the plan. But God appeared to Nathan and nixed the plan—David had too much blood on his hands from his warring to build the temple. His son would complete the task. However, God offered David more than he dared to ask for. God initiated a covenant with David and promised David that his royal line would last forever.

The entire passage hinges on the word "build" in verse 4. David would not build God's house. But God would build a dynasty out of David's house.

GRAPPLING

GOING DEEPER

Keep this in mind as you begin your fearless conversation: Look for opportunities to give to others in your group. Who can you affirm? Who can you encourage to share more?

BEHIND THE SCENES

It's significant that God sent Nathan to David to make the covenant between God and David. Nathan was the same prophet who confronted David over his adulterous relationship with Bathsheba and sending her husband on a suicide mission to avoid having to face the consequences of his sin. The presence of Nathan at both events was a quiet form of grace. It was a subtle message that God was blessing him, even though he was fully aware of David's past failures. God's favor on David's family was an unmerited act of grace on God's part. David had done nothing to earn it.

Think about everything we learned about David's life in the past weeks. In what ways might David have felt like the Big Bad Wolf—the bad influence that kept his children from connecting with God's plan for their life?

God made this promise to David—to be like a father to his children—*after* David had performed multiple sinful acts that negatively impacted his family and his kingdom. What does this tell us about God's willingness to work with all kinds of parents?

What does this passage suggest is the most important thing a parent can do to help their children live out the plan God has for their life?

God reminded David of how he dealt with him over the years. How do you think that helped David have confidence about his children's future?

INTERESTING THOUGHTS SPARKED
BY OTHERS IN MY GROUP:

GROWING

BEHIND THE SCENES

As parents it's easy to become fearful about how our children will turn out. There are so many influences in the world working to pull our children away from God. And if we're truthful, we'll admit that we bring our own sinfulness into our families. We have the potential to distract our children from truly knowing God and his will for us.

BEHIND THE SCENES

First Chronicles 17:1-15 reminds us that through Jesus we are part of God's forever family. Like David, our descendents are part of God's kingdom regardless of our actions. God's family and kingdom are established forever.

What is your biggest fear concerning your child's future? The future of the next generation? How can you bring this fear to God?

Write your reflections here.

What current activities do you do as a family that may help introduce your children to Jesus? Are there any routines you'd like to add?

Write your ideas here.

HOW CAN WE BE FULLY FAITHFUL WHEN WE'RE FULLY FLAWED?

LESSON 11: WHAT'S MY STORY IN GOD'S EYES?

GREETING

Happiest Song:

Saddest Song:

Most Inspiring Song:

Most Romantic Song:

The most inappropriate time and place to play the world's *happiest song* would be:

The most inappropriate time and place to play the world's *saddest song* would be:

The most inappropriate time and place to play the world's most *inspiring song* would be:

The most inappropriate time and place to play the world's most *romantic song* would be:

GROUNDING

God's Word: Psalm 30

A psalm. A song. For the dedication of the Temple. Of David.

> [1] I will exalt you, Lord,
>> for you lifted me out of the depths
>> and did not let my enemies gloat over me.
> [2] Lord my God, I called to you for help,
>> and you healed me.
> [3] You, Lord, brought me up from the realm of the dead;
>> you spared me from going down to the pit.
>
> [4] Sing the praises of the Lord, you his faithful people;
>> praise his holy name.
> [5] For his anger lasts only a moment,
>> but his favor lasts a lifetime;
> weeping may stay for the night,
>> but rejoicing comes in the morning.
>
> [6] When I felt secure, I said,
>> "I will never be shaken."

⁷Lord, when you favored me,
   you made my royal mountain stand firm;
but when you hid your face,
   I was dismayed.

⁸To you, Lord, I called;
   to the Lord I cried for mercy:
⁹"What is gained if I am silenced,
   if I go down to the pit?
Will the dust praise you?
   Will it proclaim your faithfulness?
¹⁰Hear, Lord, and be merciful to me;
   Lord, be my help."

¹¹You turned my wailing into dancing;
   you removed my sackcloth and clothed me with joy,
¹²that my heart may sing your praises and not be silent.
   Lord my God, I will praise you forever.

What are the first questions that come to mind? What poetic imagery in the psalm moves you?

Capture those thoughts here.

BEHIND THE SCENES

Psalm 30 is the final psalm in a string of psalms used to dedicate Solomon's temple. What's surprising about this block (Psalms 23-30) is that the majority of psalms are "lament" psalms. A lament psalm empowers the worshipper to unload their complaints and grievances to God. In the United States, the musical genre which comes closest to lament psalms is the blues. The modern reader might expect a different musical selection for an occasion as holy as the dedication of the Temple—something grand and anthemic, something that celebrated God for his greatness. At first blush, lament psalms seem to be out of place. That is until we consider God is telling us something about the type of worship he desires. Centuries later, Jesus explicitly stated that God wants worshippers who approach God in "spirit and truth." Jesus spoke plainly, while the song selection for the dedication ceremony whispers the same truth: God wants us to engage him with our real selves, even if our current circumstances have left us broken and unhappy.

Psalm 30 unfolds in four sections. The psalmist praises God for delivering him from an illness that threatened his life (verses 1-3), he calls the congregation to join him in his praise (verses 4-5), he recounts the insecurity he had felt during his illness (verses 6-10), and then finally he returns to a note praise, worshipping God for his healing (verses 11-12).

GRAPPLING

GOING DEEPER

Learning involves listening. Commit to listening to others so you can learn more about the Bible from your friends. When we commit to sharpening our listening skills, we produce conversations that are deep with meaning.

BEHIND THE SCENES

The opening of the psalm is filled with picturesque language. Psalms 27 and 30 are closely tied together. In Psalm 27, God exalts the psalmist and sets his feet on a high rock (verse 5). Now, the psalmist declares his intention to exalt God by remembering his past saving works. He wants to lift God up, because God has "lifted [him] out of the depths" (verse 1). This is the same language used when talking about pulling a bucket out of a deep well. God had pulled the psalmist out of "the realm of the dead" (verse 3), *Sheol* as the Hebrews referred to their sketchy and nebulous understanding of the afterlife. The psalmist doesn't describe the nature of his illness, but verse 5 seems to indicate he believes his particular affliction is judgment for a sin he committed. When he calls the congregation to worship God, he does so with confidence that God's anger will not last forever. God disciplines his saints, but even so, his favor rests with his saints for a lifetime. The anguish of heartfelt grieving is real, but it is also temporary. Night must yield to day, and for those who are God's, tears must yield to joy.

Review Psalm 30. Examine how David felt at different points during the psalm. How would you describe David's mood? Was he happy, sad, angry, reflective? Determine how you think David was feeling in each of the following verse sections.

Verses 1-3:

Verses 4-5:

Verses 6-10:

Verses 11-12:

Why do you think such an angst-filled song was used for the dedication of the Temple? What clues does this give us to the purpose of worship?

In verse 9, what is the basis of the psalmist's appeal for God to spare his life? What does this tell you about God's priorities regarding the story of your life?

BEHIND THE SCENES

The Old Testament concept of the afterlife, or *Sheol,* was grim, shadowy, and purposeless. It was believed to be a place without strong emotions, such as love or hate. There is no work, thought, or knowledge. Its inhabitants have no memory, can't think or praise God. In short it's a place without purpose or meaning. This is the basis of the psalmist's appeal: If he is allowed to perish into *Sheol,* the story of his life will lose its highest meaning: worshipping God.

INTERESTING THOUGHTS SPARKED BY OTHERS IN MY GROUP:

BEHIND THE SCENES

The fact that this psalm was used to dedicate the Temple creates an interesting tension. The Temple was the place where God and Israel agreed to meet each other for the purpose of worship, and this psalm is filled with angst and struggling with God.

What does this psalm tell us about having fearless conversations with God during worship?

GROWING

Does suffering tend to remind you to praise God or does it tend to push you away from God?

Write your thoughts here.

Think of a time God led you through a difficult challenge. How does that experience give you opportunity to share God's goodness with someone else?

Write your thoughts here.

What's one step you can take to be more intentional about giving God praise?

Write your idea here.

HOW CAN WE BE FULLY FAITHFUL WHEN WE'RE FULLY FLAWED?

LESSON 12: WHAT DOES GOD WANT MY LEGACY TO BE?

GREETING

What kind of legacy did Steve Jobs leave behind for us?

What legacy did Martin Luther King Jr. leave our country?

What are some other examples of people who left a positive legacy on our lives today?

Who is a person who left a legacy that made a strong, positive contribution to your life?

PARTICIPANT GUIDE

Who are the people in your life whom you want to leave a legacy for? You don't need to be a parent to answer this question. We can leave legacies in our neighborhoods, colleges, churches, friendships, and workplaces.

Now think about the people you mentioned. What do you want these people to say about the legacy you left in their life?

Write your answers in the suitcase below to symbolize you're packing them away for the future.

GROUNDING

God's Word: 1 Chronicles 28:1-20

[1] David summoned all the officials of Israel to assemble at Jerusalem: the officers over the tribes, the commanders of the divisions in the service of the king, the commanders of thousands and commanders of hundreds, and the officials in charge of all the property and livestock belonging to the king and his sons, together with the palace officials, the warriors and all the brave fighting men.

[2] King David rose to his feet and said: "Listen to me, my fellow Israelites, my people. I had it in my heart to build a house as a place of rest for the ▶

ark of the covenant of the Lord, for the footstool of our God, and I made plans to build it. [3] But God said to me, 'You are not to build a house for my Name, because you are a warrior and have shed blood.'

[4] "Yet the Lord, the God of Israel, chose me from my whole family to be king over Israel forever. He chose Judah as leader, and from the tribe of Judah he chose my family, and from my father's sons he was pleased to make me king over all Israel. [5] Of all my sons—and the Lord has given me many—he has chosen my son Solomon to sit on the throne of the kingdom of the Lord over Israel. [6] He said to me: 'Solomon your son is the one who will build my house and my courts, for I have chosen him to be my son, and I will be his father. [7] I will establish his kingdom forever if he is unswerving in carrying out my commands and laws, as is being done at this time.'

[8] "So now I charge you in the sight of all Israel and of the assembly of the Lord, and in the hearing of our God: Be careful to follow all the commands of the Lord your God, that you may possess this good land and pass it on as an inheritance to your descendants forever.

[9] "And you, my son Solomon, acknowledge the God of your father, and serve him with wholehearted devotion and with a willing mind, for the Lord searches every heart and understands every desire and every thought. If you seek him, he will be found by you; but if you forsake him, he will reject you forever. [10] Consider now, for the Lord has chosen you to build a house as the sanctuary. Be strong and do the work."

[11] Then David gave his son Solomon the plans for the portico of the temple, its buildings, its storerooms, its upper parts, its inner rooms and the place of atonement. [12] He gave him the plans of all that the Spirit had put in his mind for the courts of the temple of the Lord and all the surrounding rooms, for the treasuries of the temple of God and for the treasuries for the dedicated things. [13] He gave him instructions for the divisions of the priests and Levites, and for all the work of serving in the temple of the Lord, as well as for all the articles to be used in its service. [14] He designated the weight of gold for all the gold articles to be used in various kinds of service, and the weight of silver for all the silver articles

to be used in various kinds of service: [15] the weight of gold for the gold lampstands and their lamps, with the weight for each lampstand and its lamps; and the weight of silver for each silver lampstand and its lamps, according to the use of each lampstand; [16] the weight of gold for each table for consecrated bread; the weight of silver for the silver tables; [17] the weight of pure gold for the forks, sprinkling bowls and pitchers; the weight of gold for each gold dish; the weight of silver for each silver dish; [18] and the weight of the refined gold for the altar of incense. He also gave him the plan for the chariot, that is, the cherubim of gold that spread their wings and overshadow the ark of the covenant of the Lord.

[19] "All this," David said, "I have in writing as a result of the Lord's hand on me, and he enabled me to understand all the details of the plan."

[20] David also said to Solomon his son, "Be strong and courageous, and do the work. Do not be afraid or discouraged, for the Lord God, my God, is with you. He will not fail you or forsake you until all the work for the service of the temple of the Lord is finished.

What are the first questions that come to mind? What speaks to your heart? How do you see David leaving a legacy for Solomon and the people in his kingdom?

Capture those thoughts here.

BEHIND THE SCENES

Today's passage is part of King David's last public discourse to his people. David had aspired to build a temple for God. God, however, denied that request because David was a man of warfare. Instead, God promised him that one of his sons would be permitted to do that work instead. Upon hearing the news, David could have simply set the project down and focused on other things. Instead, David committed himself to "set the table" for his son Solomon to be able to do this work well.

David began collecting building supplies that would be needed: cut stones, iron, and cedar timbers. He built alliances with foreign kingdoms that could supply Solomon with the building materials and craftsmanship know-how that would need needed to complete the project (1 Chronicles 22:2-5).

Now in chapter 28, David gathers all the officials of the kingdom to share his vision for the construction of the temple. Solomon would not be able to build the temple on the strength of his own leadership; he was young and utterly inexperienced at leadership. He would need his key leaders to buy into the project as well.

But most importantly, David gave Solomon a spiritual legacy. He stressed the importance of maintaining a vital spiritual life. While it was true that David's kingdom would last forever, Solomon's tenure wasn't guaranteed. If Solomon forsook God, God reserved the right to take his kingdom and give it to another in David's line (verse 9).

GRAPPLING

GOING DEEPER

Think about the person whose legacy made a mark on you. How did those conversations leave you *feeling?* How could you use this time of conversation to make those around you feel the same way?

Imagine you're Solomon. What type of feelings do you have toward your father when you return home after this meeting?

If David hadn't called this meeting, how would Solomon's task have been different?

How did the legacy David left Solomon positively impact all of Israel?

BEHIND THE SCENES

One of the ways the kings of Israel were supposed to pass spiritual legacy to their successors was to have their heir write out the entirety of God's covenant with Moses by hand. They had to copy the first five books of the Bible. It was a long and tedious process, but the new king would finish the project understanding what God was like and how he expected his nation to be governed. Over time, as the spiritual health of the kingdom worsened, this practice was abandoned. But the structure was in place for spiritual legacy to be passed on.

INTERESTING THOUGHTS SPARKED BY OTHERS IN MY GROUP:

What responsibilities did Solomon have to "receive" David's legacy? Based on what you know about Solomon's life, how well did he embrace that legacy?

What does this tell you about the limits of legacy building? Why is it still worth it to do the work of building a legacy?

GROWING

What would be the legacy you'd leave your loved ones if you were to pass on today? Would you be happy with that?

Write your reflections here.

What work do you have ahead of you as you seek to leave behind a positive legacy? What's one simple thing you can do this week to take a step toward that goal?

Write your thoughts here.

HOW CAN WE BE FULLY FAITHFUL WHEN WE'RE FULLY FLAWED?

LESSON 13: WHY DOES IT FEEL LIKE GOD SOMETIMES DOESN'T KEEP THE PROMISES MADE IN THE BIBLE?

GREETING

How did you feel the moment you realized the promise you wrote down wouldn't be kept?

How did your relationship change with the person who failed to keep that promise?

What does it take to rebuild trust in a relationship after it's been violated?

Are there ever any circumstances where someone might feel like God has broken a promise he made to them? What might that do to a person's relationship with God?

GROUNDING

God's Word: Psalm 1

[1] Blessed is the one
    who does not walk in step with the wicked
or stand in the way that sinners take
    or sit in the company of mockers,
[2] but whose delight is in the law of the Lord,
    and who meditates on his law day and night.
[3] That person is like a tree planted by streams of water,
    which yields its fruit in season
and whose leaf does not wither—
    whatever they do prospers.

[4] Not so the wicked!
    They are like chaff
    that the wind blows away.
[5] Therefore the wicked will not stand in the judgment,
    nor sinners in the assembly of the righteous.

[6] For the Lord watches over the way of the righteous,
    but the way of the wicked leads to destruction.

What questions come to your mind? What advice or comfort do you receive from this psalm? What catches your attention?

Capture those thoughts here.

BEHIND THE SCENES

At first blush, it appears that Psalm 1 would have a more natural home in the book of Proverbs than in a collection of worship songs. Psalm 1 is a wisdom poem filled with themes indigenous to Proverbs. The poem is concerned with the impact the company we keep has on our character. The poem presents the choice between becoming a wise person or a person who scoffs at God's order. The poet makes a strong contrast between two sources of wisdom that every person must choose between when making life decisions: "The law of the Lord"—which David's readers would have understood as the books of Moses—or the counsel of the wicked.

So the editor chose this psalm to open the collection as a way of reminding the faithful worshippers in Israel that despite all appearances, God would ultimately provide justice for the wicked.

GRAPPLING

GOING DEEPER

The Apostle Paul once said the goal of his instruction to Timothy was love from a pure heart, a sincere faith, and a clean conscience. He left out "more head knowledge." Remember to gauge the value of this session by whether you were challenged to be more like Jesus or not.

BEHIND THE SCENES

The Prophet Jeremiah used plant metaphors to compare and contrasts the wicked and the righteous in Jeremiah 17:6-8. He describes the person who trusts in his own strength to get through life as a malnourished shrub struggling for existence in a parched salt land. But he says the person who trusts in God is like a tree planted by water that is able to withstand the season of drought. Neither the psalmist nor Jeremiah pretends that the act of trusting God exempts a person from difficult season of life. More than that, the psalmist describes the wicked as starting out looking like they are flourishing. The driest of chaff starts out being lusciously green grass. The implication for the righteous is that before God brings the justice described in Psalm 1:5-6, there will be a period of time when it will appear that the scales of God's justice are imbalanced. The psalm demands God's righteous people practice patience and trust that God is a righteous judge who will make all things right in his perfect timing.

What past questions have you had of God when you've endured hardships? Are these the same questions you have as you endure hardships today?

What hope might this psalm stir up within you during times of hardship?

How might this psalm encourage someone who felt like God wasn't keeping his promise to reward the righteous and judge the wicked?

INTERESTING THOUGHTS SPARKED
BY OTHERS IN MY GROUP:

GROWING

Where in your life does it feel like God isn't keeping his promises to you? What negative feelings about God has this generated in you?

Write your reflections here.

What would it look like for you to practice patience with God and to trust his timing? What disciplines could you build into your life to help you?

Write your thoughts here.

As we complete this quarter, let's also reflect on the theme question, "How can we be fully faithful when we're fully flawed?" Based on what you've discovered this quarter, what's one sentence that might answer that question?